D1134918

Fastened Like Nails:

WORDS OF THE WISE.
VOLUME I.

By
F. W. Boreham

1483-1662

LAMPLIGHTER
Publishing

Fastened Like Nails, Volume 1: Words of the Wise.
Copyright © 2016.
All rights reserved.
First Printing, November 2016
Fifth Printing, December 2021

Published by Lamplighter Publishing; a division of Lamplighter Ministries
International. Printed at Lamplighter Bindery, Mount Morris, NY.

The Lamplighter Collection is a family collection of rare books from the
17th, 18th and 19th centuries. Each edition is printed in an attractive hard-
bound collector's format. For more information, call us at 1-888-A-GOSPEL
(1-888-246-7735), 1-570-585-1314, visit us at *www.lamplighter.net* or write:

Lamplighter Publishing
23 State Street
Mount Morris, NY 14510

Author: F. W. Boreham
Executive Editor: Mark Hamby
Chief Editor: Deborah Hamby
Copy Editor: Darlene Catlett
Layout and Design: Bridgette Heap
Cover Design: Lorraine Larsen

ISBN10: 1-58474-247-X
ISBN13: 978-1-58474-247-0
EFSkiver3304, Burnish

From *A Bunch of Everlastings* ©1920: Oliver Cromwell, John Knox, Hugh
Latimer, and Martin Luther
From *A Temple of Topaz* ©1928: William Tyndale
From *A Faggot of Torches* ©1926: Blaise Pascal
Biographies from *A Frank Boreham Treasury* ©1984 The Moody Bible
Institute of Chicago, compilation Peter F. Gunther

Publisher's note: The rules of punctuation, spelling, and even sentence
structure of the 1800s were different than our present-day standards. We
have chosen to keep the original format as much as possible, editing only
when deemed necessary.

Preface.

Some books radically change the way a person thinks, not just for the moment, but for the rest of their life. *Fastened Like Nails*, the first volume in a collection of Frank Boreham's writings, is just such a book. Ironically, this book sat for over twenty years gathering dust on my bookshelf since I initially dismissed it as peripheral reading which I didn't have time for. However, my misconceptions were shattered during the 2015 Lamplighter Guild when our keynote speaker, Dr. Ravi Zacharias, began quoting Boreham's words of wisdom during his morning address. As it turned out, Dr. Zacharias considers Boreham to be one of the most important writers and theologians that he knows of.

Upon hearing this I was immediately reminded of the book that had been sitting on my bookshelf for decades—unread. As soon as the Guild concluded I dashed to my personal library to see if this was the book that Ravi had referenced in his lecture. I was thrilled to discover that this was indeed the book in question and proceeded to read it enthusiastically. And I was not disappointed; of the hundreds of books I have read in the last decade, I would place this one in the top ten. What intrigued me the most was seeing the way in which the power of God's Word influenced the lives of men like Luther, Latimer, Tyndall, Knox, Pascal, and Cromwell. I was surprised to find out that none of these men were genuinely committed to serving Christ until they had been deeply convicted by the Word of God, usually by a single passage.

The historical background woven into these narratives makes each story full of life, color, and beauty while also portraying the realities of tragedy and sacrifice. It is my hope that these words inspire in readers an insatiable desire to encounter the Word for themselves, the Logos that never returns void. This is a powerful book that you will read more than once and will want to share with many, especially those who "have a form of godliness but deny the power thereof." May you be as blessed as I was as you read this great work.

Mark Hamby
Hebrews 4:12

Contents.

Fastened Like Nails:

WORDS OF THE WISE.
VOLUME I.

MARTIN LUTHER'S TEXT.
(1483-1546)

Martin Luther led the Protestant Reformation and made an important contribution to German literature with his translation of the Bible. He wrote more than four hundred works, from pamphlets to large books. He arranged a new order of church services as well as a new system of church government. He wrote catechisms for the common people and introduced singing by the congregation. Of the 125 hymns that he wrote, the best known is "Ein Feste Burg" ("A Mighty Fortress").

His text: "The just shall live by his faith" (Habakkuk 2:4).

I.

It goes without saying that the text that made Martin Luther made history with a vengeance. When, through its mystical but mighty ministry, Martin Luther entered into newness of life, the face of the world was changed. It was as though all the windows of Europe had been suddenly thrown open, and the sunshine came streaming in everywhere. The destinies of empires were turned that day into a new channel. Carlyle has a stirring and dramatic chapter in which he shows that every nation under heaven stood or fell according to the attitude that it assumed towards Martin Luther. "I call this Luther a true Great Man," he exclaims. "He is great in intellect, great in courage, great in affection and integrity; one of our most lovable and gracious men. He is great, not as a hewn obelisk is great, but as an Alpine mountain is great; so simple, honest, spontaneous; not setting himself up to be great, but there for quite another purpose than the purpose of being great!" "A mighty man," he says again; "what were all emperors, popes and potentates in comparison? His light was to flame as a beacon over long centuries and epochs of the world; the whole world and its history was waiting for this man!" And elsewhere he declares that the moment in which Luther defied the wrath of the Diet of Worms was the greatest moment in the modern history of men. Here, then, was the man; what was the text that made him?

II.

Let us visit a couple of very interesting European libraries! And here, in the Convent Library at Erfurt, we are shown an exceedingly famous and beautiful picture. It represents Luther as a young monk of four and twenty, poring in the early morning over a copy of the Scriptures to which a bit of broken chain is hanging. The dawn is stealing through the open lattice, illumining both the open Bible and the eager face of its reader. And on the page that the young monk so intently studies are to be seen the words:

"The just shall live by faith."
"The just shall live by faith!"
"The just shall live by faith!"

These, then, are the words that made the world all over again. And now, leaving the Convent Library at Erfurt, let us visit another library, the Library of Rudolstadt! For here, in a glass case, we shall discover a manuscript that will fascinate us. It is a letter in the handwriting of Dr. Paul Luther, the reformer's youngest son. "In the year 1544," we read, "my late dearest father, in the presence of us all, narrated the whole story of his journey to Rome. He acknowledged with great joy that, in that city, through the Spirit of Jesus Christ, he had come to the knowledge of the truth of the everlasting gospel. It happened in this way. As he repeated his prayers on the Lateran staircase, the words of the Prophet Habakkuk came suddenly to his mind: *'The just shall live by faith.'* Thereupon he ceased his prayers, returned to Wittenberg, and took this as the chief foundation of all his doctrine."

"The just shall live by faith!"
"The just shall live by faith!"

The picture in the one library, and the manuscript in the other, have told us all that we desire to know.

III.

"The just shall live by faith!"
"The just shall live by faith!"

The words do not flash or glitter. Like the ocean, they do not give any indication upon the surface of the profundities and mysteries that lie concealed beneath. And yet of what other text can it be said that, occurring in the Old Testament, it is thrice quoted in the New?

"The just shall live by faith!" cries the Prophet.

"The just shall live by faith!" says Paul, when he addresses a letter to the greatest of the European churches.

"The just shall live by faith!" he says again, in his letter to the greatest of the Asiatic churches.

"The just shall live by faith!" says the writer of the Epistle to the Hebrews, addressing himself to Jews.

It is as though it were the sum and substance of everything, to be proclaimed by prophets in the old dispensation, and echoed by apostles in the new; to be translated into all languages and transmitted to every section of the habitable earth. Indeed, Bishop Lightfoot as good as says that the words represent the concentration and epitome of all revealed religion. "The whole law," he says, "was given to Moses in six hundred and thirteen precepts. David, in the fifteenth Psalm, brings them all within the compass of eleven. Isaiah reduces them to six; Micah to three; and Isaiah, in a later passage, to two. But Habakkuk condenses them all into one: *'The just shall live by faith!'"*

And this string of monosyllables that sums up everything and is sent to everybody—the old world's text: the new world's text: the prophet's text: the Jew's text: the European's text: the Asiatic's text: everybody's text—is, in a special and peculiar sense, Martin Luther's text. We made that discovery in the libraries of Erfurt and Rudolstadt; and we shall, as we proceed, find abundant evidence to confirm us in that conclusion.

IV.

For, strangely enough, the text that echoed itself three times in the New Testament, echoed itself three times also in the experience of Luther. It met him at Wittenberg, it met him at Bologna, and it finally mastered him at Rome.

It was at Wittenberg that the incident occurred which we have already seen transferred to the painter's canvas. In the retirement of his quiet cell, while the world is still wrapped in slumber, he pores over the epistle to the Romans. Paul's quotation from Habakkuk strangely captivates him.

"The just shall live by faith!"
"The just shall live by faith!"

"This precept," says the historian, "fascinates him. 'For the just, then,' he says to himself, 'there is a life different from that of other men; and this life is the gift of faith!' This promise, to which he opens all his heart, as if God had placed it there specially for him, unveils to him the mystery of the Christian life. For years afterwards, in the midst of his numerous occupations, he fancies that he still hears the words repeating themselves to him over and over again."

"The just shall live by faith!"
"The just shall live by faith!"

Years pass. Luther travels. In the course of his journey, he crosses the Alps, is entertained at a Benedictine Convent at Bologna, and is there overtaken by a serious sickness. His mind relapses into utmost darkness and dejection. To die thus, under a burning sky and in a foreign land! He shudders at the thought. The sense of his sinfulness troubles him; the prospect of judgement fills him with dread. But at the very moment at which these terrors reach their highest pitch, the words that had already struck him at Wittenberg recur forcibly to his memory and enlighten his soul like a ray from heaven—

'The just shall live by faith!'
'The just shall live by faith!'

Thus restored and comforted," the record concludes, "he soon regains his health and resumes his journey."

The third of these experiences—the experience narrated in that fireside conversation of which the manuscript at Rudolstadt has told us—befalls him at Rome. "Wishing to obtain an indulgence promised by the Pope to all who shall ascend Pilate's Staircase on their knees, the good Saxon monk is painfully creeping up those steps which, he is told, were miraculously transported from Jerusalem to Rome. Whilst he is performing this meritorious act, however, he thinks he hears a voice of thunder crying, as at Wittenberg and Bologna—

'The just shall live by faith!'
'The just shall live by faith!'

"These words, that twice before have struck him like the voice of an angel from heaven, resound unceasingly and powerfully within him. He rises in amazement from the steps up which he is dragging his body: he shudders at himself: he is ashamed at seeing to what a depth superstition plunged him. He flies far from the scene of his folly."

Thus, thrice in the New Testament and thrice in the life of Luther, the text speaks with singular appropriateness and effect.

V.

"This powerful text," remarks Merle D'Aubigne, "has a mysterious influence on the life of Luther. It was a *creative sentence*, both for the reformer and for the Reformation. It was in these words that God then said, 'Let there be light!' and there was light!"

VI.

It was the unveiling of the Face of God! Until this great transforming text flashed its light into the soul of Luther, his thought of God was a pagan thought. And the pagan thought

is an unjust thought, an unworthy
thought, a cruel thought. Look at this
Indian devotee! From head to foot he
bears the marks of the torture that
he has inflicted upon his body in his
frantic efforts to give pleasure to his
god. His back is a tangle of scars.
The flesh has been lacerated by the
pitiless hooks by which he has swung
himself on the terrible churuka. Iron
spears have been repeatedly run
through his tongue. His ears are torn
to ribbons. What does it mean? It can
only mean that he worships a fiend!
His god loves to see him in anguish!
His cries of pain are music in the ears
of the deity whom he adores! This
ceaseless orgy of torture is his futile
endeavour to satisfy the idol's lust
for blood. Luther made precisely the
same mistake. To his sensitive mind,
every thought of God was a thing of
terror. "When I was young," he tells
us, "it happened that at Eisleben, on
Corpus Christi day, I was walking

with the procession, when, suddenly, the sight of the Holy Sacrament which was carried by Doctor Staupitz, so terrified me that a cold sweat covered my body and I believed myself dying of terror." All through his convent days he proceeds upon the assumption that God gloats over his misery. His life is a long drawn out agony. He creeps like a shadow along the galleries of the cloister, the walls echoing with his dismal moanings. His body wastes to a skeleton; his strength ebbs away: on more than one occasion his brother monks find him prostrate on the convent floor and pick him up for dead. And all the time he thinks of God as One who can find delight in these continuous torments! The just shall live, he says to himself, by penance and by pain. The just shall live by fasting: the just shall live by fear.

VII.

"The just shall live by fear!" Luther mutters to himself every day of his life.

"The just shall live by faith!" says the text that breaks upon him like a light from heaven.

"By fear! By fear!"

"By faith! By faith!"

And what is faith? The theologians may find difficulty in defining it, yet every little child knows what it is. In all the days of my own ministry I have found only one definition that has satisfied me, and whenever I have had occasion to speak of faith, I have recited it. It is Bishop O'Brien's:—

"They who know what is meant by faith in a promise, know what is meant by faith in the Gospel; they who know what is meant by faith in a remedy, know what is meant by faith in the blood of the Redeemer; they who know

what is meant by faith in a physician, faith in an advocate, faith in a friend, know, too, what is meant by faith in the Lord Jesus Christ."

With the coming of the text, Luther passes from the realm of fear into the realm of faith. It is like passing from the rigours of an arctic night into the sunshine of a summer day; it is like passing from a crowded city slum into the fields where the daffodils dance and the linnets sing; it is like passing into a new world; it is like *entering Paradise!*

VIII.

Yes, it is like *entering Paradise!* The expression is his, not mine. "Before those words broke upon my mind," he says, "I hated God and was angry with Him because, not content with frightening us sinners by the law and by the miseries of life, he

still further increased our torture by
the gospel. But when, by the Spirit of
God, I understood these words—

'The just shall live by faith!'
'The just shall live by faith!'
—then I felt born again like a new
man; I entered through the open doors
into *the very Paradise of God!*"

"Henceforward," he says again, "I
saw the beloved and holy Scriptures
with other eyes. The words that I had
previously detested, I began from
that hour to value and to love as the
sweetest and most consoling words in
the Bible. In very truth, this text was
to me *the true gate of Paradise!*"

*"An open door into the very
Paradise of God!"*

*"This text was to me the true gate
of Paradise!"*

And they who enter into the City of
God by that gate will go no more out
for ever.

Hugh Latimer's Text.
(c. 1485-1555)

Hugh Latimer was a martyr of the Protestant Reformation in England. He studied at Cambridge University and became a priest, named chaplain of King Henry VIII. Later he became bishop of Worcester. He refused to sign the king's six articles, which he believed represented a return of England to Catholicism, and as a result was confined to the Tower of London and later imprisoned there by Queen Mary. He and Nicholas Ridley were burned at the stake along with nearly 300 other Protestant leaders under Queen Mary.

His text: "This is a faithful saying, and worthy of all acceptation, that Christ Jesus came into the world to save sinners, of whom I am chief" (I Timothy 1:15).

I.

THERE is excitement in the streets of London! Who is this upon whom the crowd is pressing as he passes down the Strand? Women throw open the windows and gaze admiringly out; shopkeepers rush from behind their counters to join the throng as it approaches; apprentices fling aside their tools and, from every lane and alley, pour into the street; waggoners rein in their horses and leave them for a moment unattended; the taverns empty as the procession draws near them! Everybody is anxious to catch a glimpse of this man's face; to hear, if possible, the sound of his voice; or, better still, to clasp his hand as he passes. For this is Hugh Latimer; the terror of evil-doers; the idol of the common people; and, to use the phraseology of a chronicler of the period, "the honestest man in England." By sheer force of character he has raised himself from a ploughman's cottage to a bishop's palace—an achievement that, in the sixteenth century, stands without precedent or parallel. "My father was a yeoman," he says, in the course of a sermon preached before the King, "my father was a yeoman, and had no lands of his own; he had a farm of three or four pounds a year at the utmost, and hereupon he tilled so much as kept half-a-dozen men. He had walk for a hundred sheep; and my mother milked thirty kine. He kept me at school, or else I had not been able to have preached before the King's majesty now." Nor has his elevation spoiled him. He has borne with him in his exaltations the spirit of the common people. He feels as they feel; he thinks as they think; he even speaks as they speak. It was said of him, as of his Master, that the common people heard him gladly. In cathedral pulpits and royal chapels he speaks a dialect that the common people can readily understand; he uses homely illustrations gathered from the farm, the kitchen and the counting-house;

he studiously eschews the pedantries of the schoolmen and the subtleties of the theologians. His sermons are, as Macaulay says, "the plain talk of a plain man, who sprang from the body of the people, who sympathised strongly with their wants and their feelings, and who boldly uttered their opinions." It was on account of the fearless way in which stout-hearted old Hugh exposed the misdeeds of men in ermine tippets and gold collars that the Londoners cheered him as he walked down the Strand to preach at Whitehall, struggled for a touch of his gown, and bawled, "Have at them, Father Latimer!" There he goes, then; a man of sound sense, honest affection, earnest purpose and sturdy speech; a man whose pale face, stooping figure and emaciated frame show that it has cost him something to struggle upwards from the ploughshare to the palace; a man who looks for all the world like some old Hebrew prophet transplanted incongruously into the prosaic life of London! He passes down the Strand with the people surging fondly around him. He loves the people, and is pleased with their confidence in him. His heart is simple enough and human enough to find the sweetest of all music in the plaudits that are ringing in his ears. So much for London; we must go to Oxford!

II.

There is excitement in the streets of Oxford! Who is this upon whom the crowd is pressing as he passes down from the Mayor's house to the open ground in front of Balliol College? Again, women are leaning out of the windows; shopkeepers are forsaking their counters; apprentices are throwing aside their tools; and drivers are deserting their horses that they may stare at him. It is Hugh Latimer again! He is a little thinner than when we saw him in London; for he has exchanged a palace for a prison. The people still press upon him and make progress difficult; but this time they crowd around him that they may curse him! It is the old story of "Hosannah!" one day and "Away with Him! Crucify Him!" the next. The multitude is a fickle master. Since we saw him in the Strand, the crown has passed from one head to another; the court has changed its ways to gratify the whims of its new mistress; the Government has swung round to match the moods of the court; and the people, like sheep, have followed their leaders. They are prepared now to crown the men whom before they would have crucified, and to crucify the men whom they would then have crowned. But Hugh Latimer and his companion—for this time he is not alone—are not of the same accommodating temper. Hugh Latimer is still "the honestest man in England!" His conscience is still his

only monitor; his tongue is still free;
his soul is not for sale! And so—

In Oxford town the faggots they piled,
With furious haste and with curses wild,
Round two brave men of our British breed,
Who dared to stand true to their speech and deed;
Round two brave men of that sturdy race,
Who with tremorless souls the worst can face;
Round two brave souls who could keep their tryst
Through a pathway of fire to follow Christ.
And the flames leaped up, but the blinding smoke
Could not the soul of Hugh Latimer choke;
For, said he, "Brother Ridley, be of good cheer,
A candle in England is lighted here,
Which by grace of God shall never go out!"—
And that speech in whispers was echoed about—
Latimer's Light shall never go out,
However the winds may blow it about.
Latimer's Light has come to stay
Till the trump of a coming judgement day.

"Bishop Ridley," so runs the
record, "first entered the lists, dressed
in his episcopal habit; and, soon after,

Bishop Latimer, dressed, as usual, in his prison garb. Master Latimer now suffered the keeper to pull off his prison-garb and then he appeared in his shroud. Being ready, he fervently recommended his soul to God, and then he delivered himself to the executioner, saying to the Bishop of London these prophetical words: 'We shall this day, my lord, light such a candle in England as shall never be extinguished!'"

But it is time that we went back forty years or so, to a time long before either of the processions that we have just witnessed took place. We must ascertain at what flame the light that kindled that candle was itself ignited.

III.

Very early in the sixteenth century, England was visited by one of the greatest scholars of the Renaissance, Desiderius Erasmus. After being welcomed with open arms at the Universities, he returned to the Continent and engrossed himself in his learned researches. At Cambridge, however, he had made a profound and indelible impression on at least one of the scholars. Thomas Bilney, familiarly known as "Little Bilney," was feeling, in a vague and indefinite way, the emptiness of the religion that he had been taught. He felt that Erasmus possessed a secret that was hidden from English eyes, and he vowed that, whatever it might cost him, he would purchase every line that came from the great master's pen. In France, Erasmus translated the New Testament into Latin. The ingenuity and industry of Bilney soon secured for him a copy of the book. As to its effect upon him, he shall speak for himself. "My soul was sick," he says, "and I longed for peace, but nowhere could I find it. I went to the priests, and they appointed me penances and pilgrimages; yet, by these things my poor sick soul was nothing profited. But at last I heard of Jesus. It was then, when first the New Testament was set forth by Erasmus, that the light came. I bought the book, being drawn thereto rather by the Latin than by the Word of God, for at that time I knew not what the Word of God meant. And, on the first reading of it, as I well remember, I chanced upon these words, *'This is a faithful saying, and worthy of all acceptation, that Christ Jesus came into the world to save sinners, of whom I am chief.'* That one sentence, through God's inward working, did so lift up my poor bruised spirit that the very bones within me leaped for joy and gladness. It was as if, after a long, dark night, day had suddenly broke!" But what has all this to do with Hugh Latimer?

IV.

In those days Latimer was preaching at Cambridge, and all who heard him fell under the spell of his transparent honesty and rugged eloquence. Latimer was then the sturdy champion of the old religion and the uncompromising foe of all who were endeavouring to introduce the new learning. Of all the friars, he was the most punctilious, the most zealous, the most devoted. Bilney went to hear him and fell in love with him at once. He saw that the preacher was mistaken; that his eyes had not been opened to the sublimities that had flooded his own soul with gladness; but he recognised his sincerity, his earnestness and his resistless power; and he longed to be the instrument of his illumination. If only he could do for Latimer what Aquila and Priscilla did for Apollos, and expound unto him the way of God more perfectly! It became the dream and desire of

Bilney's life. "O God," he cried, "I am but 'Little Bilney,' and shall never do any great thing for Thee; but give me the soul of that man, Hugh Latimer, and what wonders he shall do in Thy most holy Name!"

Where there's a will there's a way! One day, as Latimer descends from the pulpit, he passes so close to Bilney that his robes almost brush the student's face. Like a flash, a sudden inspiration leaps to Bilney's mind. "Prithee, Father Latimer," he whispers, "may I confess my soul to thee?" The preacher beckons, and, into the quiet room adjoining, the student follows.

Of all the strange stories that heartbroken penitents have poured into the ears of Father-Confessors since first the confessional was established, that was the strangest! Bilney falls on his knees at Latimer's feet and allows his soul, pent up for so long, to utter itself freely at last. He tells of the aching hunger of his heart; he tells of the visit of Erasmus; he tells of the purchase of the book; and then he tells of the text. "There it stood," he says, the tears standing in his eyes, "the very word I wanted. It seemed to be written in letters of light: *'This is a faithful saying, and worthy of all acceptation, that Christ Jesus came into the world to save sinners.'* O Father Latimer," he cries, the passion of his fervour increasing as the memory of his own experience rushes back upon him, "I went to the priests and they pointed me to broken cisterns that held no water and only mocked my thirst! I bore the load of my sins until my soul was crushed beneath the burden! And then I saw that *'Christ Jesus came into the world to save sinners, of whom I am chief'*; and now, being justified by faith, I have peace with God through our Lord Jesus Christ!"

Latimer is taken by storm. He is completely overwhelmed. He, too, knows the aching dissatisfaction that Bilney has described. He has experienced for years the same insatiable hunger, the same devouring thirst. To the astonishment of Bilney, Latimer rises and then kneels beside him. The Father-Confessor seeks guidance from his penitent! Bilney draws from his pocket the sacred volume that has brought such comfort and such rapture to his own soul. It falls open at the passage that Bilney has read to himself over and over and over again: *"This is a faithful saying, and worthy of all acceptation, that Christ Jesus came into the world to save sinners, of whom I am chief."* The light that never was on sea or shore illumines the soul of Hugh Latimer, and Bilney sees that the passionate desire of his heart has been granted him. And from that hour Bilney and Latimer lived only that they might unfold to all kinds and conditions of men the unsearchable riches of Christ.

V.

"This is a faithful saying!" That is the preacher's comfort. In the course of a recent tour through Western Australia, I was taken through the gold diggings. And, near Kanowna, I was shown the spot on which, years ago, there gathered one of the largest and most extraordinary congregations that ever assembled on this side of the world. It was whispered all over the diggings that an enormous nugget had been found and that Father Long, the local priest, had seen it and knew exactly where it was discovered. Morning, noon and night the young priest was pestered by eager gold-hunters for information; but to one and all his lips were sealed. At last he consented to announce publicly the exact locality of the wonderful find. At the hour fixed men came from far and near, some on horseback,

some on camels, some in all kinds of conveyances, and thousands on foot. It was the largest gathering of diggers in the history of the gold fields. At the appointed time Father Long appeared, surveyed the great sea of bronzed and bearded faces, and then announced that the "Sacred Nugget" had been found in the Lake Gwynne country. In a moment the crowd had vanished! There was the wildest stampede for the territory to which the priest had pointed them. But as the days passed by, the disappointed seekers, in twos and threes, came dribbing wearily back. Not a glint of gold had been seen by any of them! And then the truth flashed upon them. The priest had been hoaxed! The "Sacred Nugget" was a mass of common metal splashed with gold paint! Father Long took the matter bitterly to heart; he went to bed a broken and humiliated man; and, a few months later, disconsolate, he died! It was a great day in Hugh

Latimer's life when he got among the "faithful sayings," the sayings of which he was certain, the sayings that could never bring to any confiding hearer the heartbreak and disgust of disappointment.

VI.

"It is worthy of all acceptation!" It is worthy! It is worthy of your acceptance, your Majesty, for this proclamation craves no patronage! It is worthy of your acceptance, your Excellency, your Grace, my Lords, Ladies and Gentlemen all, for the gospel asks no favours! It is worthy, worthy, worthy of the acceptance of you all! Hugh Latimer stood before kings and courtiers, and declared that *"this is a faithful saying, and worthy of all acceptation, that Christ Jesus came into the world to save sinners."* Never once did he forget the dignity of his message: it was faithful; it was worthy

in its own right of the acceptance of the lordliest; and he himself staked his life upon it at the last!

VII.

Dr. Archibald Alexander, of Princeton, was for sixty years a minister of Christ; and for forty of those years he was a Professor of Divinity. No man in America was more revered or beloved. He died on October 22, 1851. As he lay a-dying, he was heard by a friend to say, "All my theology is reduced now to this narrow compass: *'This is a faithful saying, and worthy of all acceptation, that Christ Jesus came into the world to save sinners.'*" In life and in death Hugh Latimer was of pretty much the same mind.

WILLIAM TYNDALE'S TEXT.
(1494-1536)

William Tyndale, a contemporary of Martin Luther, was one of the great leaders of the Protestant Reformation in England. He became very proficient in the Greek language while attending the universities of Oxford and Cambridge, and studied Hebrew in Hamburg, Germany, with some prominent Jews. It was reading the Greek New Testament of Erasmus and the works of Martin Luther that caused him to want to give the Bible to the common people in their own language. He translated the New Testament into English and had it published in Worms, Germany. He also translated the Pentateuch and the book of Jonah. On October 6, 1536, Tyndale was first strangled and then burned at the stake. His last words, spoken in a loud voice, were "Lord, open the king of England's eyes!"

His text: "We love Him because He first loved us" (1 John 4:19).

I.

How heartily and incredulously Harry Walsh would have laughed if some little bird had whispered in his ear that, in centuries to come, men would speak of William Tyndale as a grave and austere scholar, a stern and gloomy reformer, a severe and unbending controversialist! And Humphrey Monmouth would have felt very similarly. For Harry Walsh, a sunny little fellow of six, living at Old Sodbury, and Humphrey Monmouth, an alderman and well-known merchant of the city of London, knew Mr. Tyndale as one of the most winsome, one of the most genial, and one of the most lovable of men. Their happiest hours were spent in his society. Harry was the elder son of Sir John Walsh, a knight of Gloucestershire, and Mr. Tyndale was his private tutor. Here they are, sitting together beside a stile under a giant chestnut-tree, surveying from this green and graceful hillside the quaint little hamlet nestling in the hollow! Harry, in all the bravery of his trim velvet suit, with silk stockings and silver buckles, is perched on the top of the stile. His tutor, a young man of thirty, of well-knit frame and thoughtful but pleasant face, with nut-brown hair and deep-set hazel eyes, is seated on the footstep below him. A little brown squirrel eyes them suspiciously from a branch overhead, and a cuckoo is calling from the copse near by. Harry carries an armful of bluebells.

"What wonderful times we are living in!" exclaims Mr. Tyndale, his eyes sparkling with enthusiasm. "Why, you and I ought to thank God every day, Harry, that He has sent us into the world just now! Every morning brings news of some fresh wonder!"

It was no exaggeration. The air literally tingled with sensation and romance. It was an age of thrills! The world was being made all over again. Civilisation was being overhauled and recast. The very planet was assuming a fresh shape. One day Bartholomew Diaz added Africa to the map of the world; the next, Columbus added America; and then Vasco da Gama unveiled India to the eyes of Europe. Continents were springing up like mushrooms on a misty morning. And fresh continents produced fresh oceans. Twenty years after Columbus sailed across the Atlantic, Nunez de Balboa

> ... with eagle eyes
> First stared at the Pacific—and all his men
> Looked at each other with a wild surmise—
> Silent, upon a peak in Darien.

Navigation was the fever of the hour. The vast oceans, so long a waste of loneliness, became a snowstorm of white sails. Every few days bronzed explorers seemed to be stepping from the decks of battered and weatherbeaten vessels to tell of new and astonishing discoveries in the Atlantic, in the Pacific, in the Indian Ocean—everywhere!

Nor was the land less sensational than the sea. For one thing, William Caxton was setting up his marvellous presses. Macaulay says that the invention of printing was the most notable event that took place during a thousand years of human history. It took the world by storm. Learned men, fashionable ladies, and great nobles thronged Caxton's little printing-house to see how the miracle was performed; whilst less intelligent people declined to go near it, declaring that such results could only be achieved by witchery, necromancy, and illicit commerce with evil spirits.

Moreover, to add to the wonder of it all, the printing-press came into the world at the very moment when the world had something worth printing. For it was the age of the Renaissance and the Reformation! Whilst Columbus was revealing a new world in the West, Copernicus was opening up a new universe in the skies, and Martin Luther was arousing a thousand thunders by tearing down the curtain that intervened between the common people and the Kingdom of Heaven. Faith's pilgrim path was being blazed. Astronomy was being born. Culture of all kinds was exciting boundless enthusiasm. Men were eager to think. In the realms of Religion, of Science, of Philosophy, of Music, of Art—indeed, in every department of learning—illustrious adventurers, whose names will live for ever, appeared like bright stars that twinkle suddenly out of the age-long dark. Men fell in love with the world— with this world and with every other. An infinite horizon was opened to the simplest minds. People who had lived in an age became citizens of all the ages. People who had lived in a tiny village found themselves exploring mighty continents. Lecky declares that the enlightenment and civilisation of ancient times was restricted almost entirely to great centres like Athens and Rome; it never penetrated rural districts. In the awakening that took place in Tyndale's boyhood and youth it was quite otherwise. It was in those eventful days that mysteries that had for centuries baffled the minds of sages became the gossip of every chimney-corner and the talk of every tap-room.

"What wonderful times we are living in," exclaims Mr. Tyndale, partly to himself and partly to his young charge perched on the rustic stile. Harry's golden hours are the hours that he spends rambling across the fields or through the woods in Mr. Tyndale's delightful company. For he knows that, as soon as they warm to their stride, his tutor will tell him the

latest wonder of which the coach from
London has brought word.

II.

All things come to an end,
however, as Harry discovers to his
sorrow. As long as he lived he always
declared that the deepest shadow that
darkened his happy boyhood was his
tutor's resignation. He never forgot the
evening on which Mr. Tyndale told
him that he must leave Old Sodbury.

The candles having been lit, Mr.
Tyndale, as is his custom, reads to
the two boys—Harry and Richard—a
few verses from his Greek Testament,
translating and commenting as he goes
along.

"We must read our favourite verses
to-night," he had said, with a smile of
singular sweetness in which, however,
a suspicion of sadness seemed to linger.
The boys know exactly the passage to
which he refers. They know how dear

to him are the verses that he has taught them, too, to love.

"Ye are of God, little children," he begins, and reads on till he comes to the words: *"We love Him because He first loved us."* Those words, he used to tell the boys, were the pearly gate through which he entered the Kingdom.

"I used to think," he said, "that salvation was not for me, since I did not love God; but those precious words showed me that God does not love us because we first loved Him. No, no; *'we love Him because He first loved us.'* It makes all the difference!"

The familiar passage having been read once more, Mr. Tyndale tells them that he is leaving them. The boys are soon in tears, and the tutor's gentle voice is husky.

"But why," instantly demands Richard, breaking out in a passion of childish grief, "why must you go?"

He draws them to him and attempts to explain.

"I must go," he says quietly, with one arm round the shoulders of each boy, "because I have found the work that God has sent me into the world to do. You have heard the things that have been said at dinner. Great and wise men, even preachers and prelates of the Church, come to dine with your father and mother, and say things that they could not possibly say if they knew aught of the Scriptures. If learned doctors and eloquent preachers are so ignorant of the divine Word, is it any wonder that *the people* are in darkness? A new day is dawning; the people are reading and thinking; it is time they had the Bible in their own tongue; and so, as I told your father and Dr. Hampton at dinner last night, I have resolved that, if God spare my life, I will cause every ploughboy in England to know the Scriptures better than the priests and prelates know them now. But it cannot be done here. I must go to London, and there, I trust, Bishop Tunstall will counsel and assist me."

And so, after taking a sorrowful farewell of the household at Old Sodbury, Mr. Tyndale turns his face towards London.

III.

But London receives him with a scowl. He soon discovers that he has poked his hand into a hornets' nest. On his first appearance at the palace, the bishop gives him the cold shoulder; and, when he persists in his overtures, he is threatened with all the thunderbolts that the Church can hurl. By every ship that glides up the Thames the writings of Martin Luther are being surreptitiously imported into England, and men are being hurried to prison and to death for reading them. There is nothing to indicate to the disappointed young tutor that, in centuries to come, his statue will hold a place of honour on the Victoria Embankment, and that, at its unveiling, princes and peers will bare their heads in reverence to his illustrious memory!

And yet, whilst Church and State frown upon his project and eye him with suspicion, those who come into intimate touch with him are captivated by his charm. From his old employer at Sodbury he brings letters of introduction to some of the merchant princes of the metropolis, and in their homes he soon becomes a loved and honoured guest. With Alderman Humphrey Monmouth he stayed for more than six months. On week-days he worked quietly at his translation. "But," as an old chronicler says, "when Sunday came, then went he to some merchant's house or other, whither came many other merchants, and unto them would he read some one parcel of Scripture, the which proceeded so sweetly, gently and fruitfully from him that it was a heavenly comfort to the audience to hear him read the Scriptures. He particularly loved the writings of St. John."

Harry and Richard Walsh must have smiled knowingly if that last sentence ever came under their notice: "He particularly loved the writings of St. John." They would see again the glowing face of their old tutor as he read the sentences that were so dear to him. And when he came to the words: *"We love Him because He first loved us,"* they would once more hear him tell of the way in which those priceless syllables had first impressed his soul.

Two things, however, are now clear. The first is that the people of England are hungry for the Word of God in their mother tongue; the second is that it is out of the question to attempt such a publication in London. This being so, he must brace himself for another painful wrench. Tearing himself from

the homes in which so many delightful
hours have been spent, he sets sail for
the Continent.

IV.

And, on the Continent, he knows
of at least one kindred spirit. Martin
Luther is hard at work translating
the Scriptures. "Would to God,"
Luther cried, "that this book were in
every language and in every home."
Mr. Tyndale decides to hasten to
Wittenberg and talk things over with
the man who was shaking the very
foundations of Europe. It is a pity that
we have no classical painting of that
historic meeting.

Luther and Tyndale! The German
Bible of to-day is the most enduring
and most glorious monument to Martin
Luther; the English Bible of to-day is
the most enduring and most glorious
monument to William Tyndale! And
here, in 1524, we see the two men

spending a few memorable days together!

The rest of the story is well known. We have all chuckled over the way in which Tyndale outwitted his old antagonist, the Bishop of London. The New Testament in English is at last complete. "It is called the *New Testament*," Tyndale explains, "because it is the Last Will of Jesus Christ, in which He bequeaths all His goods to those that repent and believe." But how is it to reach England? The ports are closed against it! The book is contraband! Yet, in crates and casks and cases, in boxes and barrels and bales, in rolls of cloth and sacks of flour and bundles of merchandise, the Testaments come pouring into the country!

"Very well!" retorts the bishop, "if we cannot *ban* the books, we'll *buy* the books and *burn* them!" He does so, only to discover, as soon as the flames of his famous fire have died down, that, in buying them, he has provided Tyndale with the wherewithal to print a larger and better edition!

We have all experienced the thrill of this brave, adventurous career. He was harassed; he was excommunicated; he was driven from pillar to post; he was hunted from country to country; he was shipwrecked; he was betrayed; he was imprisoned; he was tortured; and, at last, he was sentenced to a shameful death.

And we have all felt the pathos of that last letter of his. He is only fifty-six; but he is worn out and decrepit. Lying in his damp cell at Vilvorde, awaiting the stroke that is to emancipate his soul for ever, he reminds his friends that the date of his execution has not been fixed and that winter is coming on.

"Bring me," he begs, "a warmer cap, something to patch my leggings, a woollen shirt, and, *above all, my Hebrew Bible!*"

"Above all, my Bible!"

The words are eminently characteristic. He lived for the Bible; he died for the Bible; and he mounted the scaffold knowing that the Bible was being read in every chimney-corner, on every village green, and in every tavern and coffee-house in England.

V.

It is a sharp October morning in 1536. The young squire of Old Sodbury—Henry Walsh—sits by his dining-room fire with his hands in his pockets and a far-away look in his eye. His handsome young wife, entering the room, demands the cause of his unwonted abstraction. Drawing her to him, he tells her that news has just reached the village that his dear old tutor, William Tyndale, has been strangled and burned for his faith. Then, gently taking her arm, he leads her across the room, and they stand for a moment in reverent silence before the text upon the wall:

WE LOVE HIM BECAUSE
HE FIRST LOVED US.

He does not repeat the story; she has heard it from his lips so often.

JOHN KNOX'S TEXT.
(c. 1514-1572)

John Knox led the Protestant Reformation in Scotland. It was after his close friend George Wishart was burned at the stake that Knox began his career as a reformer. He was forced to serve as a galley slave for the French for nineteen months. When Catholic Queen Mary ascended the throne in 1553, Knox went into exile in Germany and Switzerland, where he became acquainted with John Calvin. The Protestant faith was adopted in Scotland as the state religion in 1560. The Parliament appointed Knox chairman of a committee that produced the First Scottish Confession of Faith *and the* First Book of Discipline, *intended to be used as standards of faith and government for the Scottish Church.*

His text: "And this is life eternal, that they might know Thee, the only true God, and Jesus Christ whom Thou has sent" (John 17:3).

I.

Some men are not born to die. It is their prerogative to live; they come on purpose. A thousand deaths will not lay them in a grave. No disease from within, no danger from without, can by any means destroy them. They bear upon their faces the stamp of the immortal. In more senses than one, they come into the world for good. Among such deathless men John Knox stands out conspicuously. When in Edinburgh it is impossible to believe that John Knox lived four hundred years ago. He is so very much alive to-day that it seems incredible that he was living even then. The people will show you his grave in the middle of the road, and the meagre epitaph on the flat tombstone will do its feeble best to convince you that his voice has been silent for centuries; but you will sceptically shake your head and move away. For, as you walk about the noble and romantic city, John Knox is everywhere! He is the most ubiquitous man you meet. You come upon him at every street corner. Here is the house in which he dwelt; there is the church in which he preached; at every turn you come upon places that are filled by him still. The very stones vibrate with the strident accents of his voice; the walls echo to his footsteps. I was introduced to quite a number of people in Edinburgh; but I blush to confess that I have forgotten them all—*all but John Knox*. It really seems to me, looking back upon that visit, that I met John Knox somewhere or other every five minutes. I could hear the ring of his voice; I could see the flash of his eye; I could feel the impress of his huge and commanding personality. The tomb in the middle of the road notwithstanding, John Knox is indisputably the most virile force in Scotland at this hour. I dare say that, like me, he sometimes catches sight of that tomb in the middle of the road. If so, he laughs—as he could laugh—and strides defiantly on. For John Knox was born in 1505 and, behold, he liveth and abideth for ever!

II.

John Knox, I say, was born in 1505. In 1505, therefore, Scotland was born again. For the birth of such a man is the regeneration of a nation. Life in Knox was not only immortal; it was contagious. Because of Knox, Carlyle affirms, the people began to live! "In the history of Scotland," says Carlyle, himself a Scotsman, "in the history of Scotland I can find but one epoch: it contains nothing of world-interest at all, but this Reformation by Knox." But surely, surely, the sage is nodding! Has Carlyle forgotten Sir Walter Scott and Robert Burns and all Scotland's noble contribution to literature, to industry, to religion and to life? But Carlyle will not retract or modify a single word. "This that Knox did for his nation," he goes on, "was a resurrection as from death. The people began to live! Scotch literature and thought, Scotch industry; James Watt, David Hume, Walter Scott, Robert Burns: I find John Knox acting in the heart's core of every one of these persons and phenomena; I find that without him they would not have been." So much have I said in order to show that, beyond the shadow of a doubt, if a text made John Knox, then that text made history.

III.

"Go!" said the old reformer to his wife, as he lay a-dying, and the words were his last, "go, read where I cast my first anchor!" She needed no more explicit instructions, for he had told her the story again and again. It is Richard

Bannatyne, Knox's serving-man, who has placed the scene on record. "On November 24, 1572," he says, "John Knox departed this life to his eternal rest. Early in the afternoon he said, 'Now, for the last time, I commend my spirit, soul and body'—pointing upon his three fingers—'into Thy hands, O Lord!' Thereafter, about five o'clock, he said to his wife, 'Go, read where I cast my first anchor!' She did not need to be told, and so she read the seventeenth of John's evangel." Let us listen as she reads it! *Thou hast given Him authority over all flesh, that He should give eternal life to as many as Thou hast given Him, and this is life eternal, that they might know Thee, the only true God, and Jesus Christ whom Thou hast sent.*

Here was a strange and striking contrast!

"Eternal Life! Life Eternal!" says the Book.

Now listen to the laboured breathing from the bed!

The Bed speaks of Death; the Book speaks of Life Everlasting!

"Life!" the dying man starts as the great cadences fall upon his ear.

"This is Life Eternal, that they might *know Thee!"*

"Life Eternal!"

"It was *there*," he declares with his last breath, "it was there that I cast my first anchor!"

IV.

How was that first anchor cast? I have tried to piece the records together. Paul never forgot the day on which he saw Stephen stoned; John Knox never forgot the day on which he saw George Wishart burned. Wishart was a man "of such grace"—so Knox himself tells us—"as before him was never heard within this realm." He was regarded with an awe that was next door to superstition, and with an affection that was almost adoration. Are we not told that in the days when the plague lay over Scotland, "the people of Dundee saw it approaching from the west in the form of a great black cloud? They fell on their knees and prayed, crying to the cloud to pass them by, but even while they prayed it came nearer. Then they looked around for the most holy man among them, to intervene with God on their behalf. All eyes turned to George Wishart, and he stood up, stretching his arms to the cloud, and prayed, and it rolled back." Out on the borders of the town, however, the pestilence was raging, and Wishart, hastening thither, took up his station on the town wall, preaching to the plague-stricken on the one side of him and to the healthy on the other, and exhibiting such courage and intrepidity in grappling with the awful scourge that he became the idol of the grateful people. In 1546, however, he was convicted of heresy and burned at the foot of the Castle Wynd, opposite the Castle Gate. When he came near to the fire, Knox tells us, he sat down upon his knees, and repeated aloud some of the most touching petitions from the Psalms. As a sign of forgiveness, he kissed the executioner on the cheek, saying: "Lo, here is a token that I forgive thee. My harte, do thine office!" The faggots were kindled, and the leaping flames bore the soul of Wishart triumphantly skywards.

V.

And there, a few yards off, stands Knox! Have a good look at him! He is a man "rather under middle height, with broad shoulders, swarthy face, black hair, and a beard of the same colour a span and a half long. He has heavy eyebrows, eyes deeply sunk, cheekbones prominent and cheeks ruddy. The mouth is large, the lips full, especially the upper one. The whole aspect of the man is not unpleasing; and, in moments of emotion, it is invested with an air of dignity and majesty." Knox could never shake from his sensitive mind the tragic yet triumphant scene near the Castle Gate; and when, many years afterwards, he himself turned aside to die, he repeated with closed eyes the prayers that he had heard George Wishart offer under the shadow of the stake.

Was it *then*, I wonder, that John Knox turned sadly homeward and read to himself the great High Priestly prayer in "the seventeenth of John's evangel"? Was it on that memorable night that he caught a glimpse of the place which all the redeemed hold in the heart of the Redeemer? Was it on that melancholy evening that there broke upon him the revelation of a love that enfolded not only his martyred friend and himself, but the faithful of every time and of every clime? Was it *then* that he opened his heart to the marvel and the music of those tremendous words: *"Thou hast given Him authority over all flesh, that He should give eternal life to as many as Thou hast given Him; and this is life eternal, that they might know Thee, the only true God, and Jesus Christ whom Thou hast sent."* Was it *then*? I cannot say for certain. I only know that we never meet with Knox in Scottish story until after the martyrdom of Wishart; and I know that, by the events of that sad and tragic day, all his soul was stirred within him. But, although I do not know for certain that the anchor was first cast *then*, I know that it was first cast *there*. "Go!" he said, with the huskiness of death upon his speech, "read me where I cast my first anchor!" And his wife straightway read to him the stately sentences I have just re-written.

"Life Eternal!"

"This is Life Eternal!"

"This is Life Eternal, that they might *know Thee!"*

"It was there, *there*, THERE, that I cast my first anchor!"

VI.

Fierce as were the storms that beat upon Knox during the great historic years that followed, that anchor bravely held. To say nothing of his experiences at Court and the powerful efforts to coax or to cow him into submission, think of those twelve years of exile, eighteen months of which were spent on the French galleys. We catch two furtive glimpses of him. The galley in which he is chained makes a cruise round the Scottish coast. It passes so near to the fair fields of Fife that Knox can distinctly see the spires of St. Andrew's. At the moment, Knox was so ill that his life was despaired of; and the taunting vision might well have broken his spirit altogether. But the anchor held; the anchor held! "Ah!" exclaimed Knox, raising himself on his elbow, "I see the steeple of that place where God first in public opened my mouth to His glory; and I am fully persuaded, how weak soever I now appear, that I shall not depart this life till that my tongue shall glorify His godly name in the same place." Again, as Carlyle tells, "a priest one day presented to the galley-slaves an image of the Virgin Mother, requiring that they, the blasphemous heretics, should do it reverence. 'Mother? Mother of God?' said Knox, when the turn came to him, 'This is no Mother of God; this is a piece of painted wood! She is better for swimming, I think, than for being worshipped!' and he flung the thing into the river." Knox had cast his anchor in the seventeenth of John's evangel.

"This is life eternal, that they might know *Thee!*"

And since he had himself found life eternal in the personal friendship of a Personal Redeemer, it was intolerable to him that others should gaze with superstitious eyes on "a bit of painted wood."

The thing fell into the river with a splash. It was a rude jest, but an expressive one. All the Reformation was summed up in it. Eternal life was not to be found in such things. *"This is life eternal, that they might know Thee!"* That, says Knox, is where I cast my first anchor; and, through all the storm and stress of those baffling and eventful years, that anchor held!

VII.

Nor was there any parting of the cable or dragging of the anchor at the last. Richard Bannatyne, sitting beside his honoured master's deathbed, heard a long, long sigh. A singular fancy overtook him.

"Now, sir," he said, "the time to end your battle has come. Remember those comfortable promises of our Saviour Jesus Christ which you have so often shown to us. And it may be that, when your eyes are blind and your ears deaf to every other sight and sound, you will still be able to recognise my voice. I shall bend over you and ask if you have still the hope of glory. Will you promise that, if you are able to give me some signal, you will do so?"

The sick man promised, and, soon after, this is what happened:

> Grim in his deep death-anguish
> the stern old champion lay,
> And the locks upon his pillow
> were floating thin and grey,
> And, visionless and voiceless,
> with quick and labouring breath,
> He waited for his exit
> through life's dark portal, Death.

"Hast thou the hope of glory?"
They bowed to catch the thrill
That through some languid token
might be responsive still,
Nor watched they long
nor waited for some obscure reply,
He raised a clay-cold finger,
and pointed to the sky.

So the death-angel found him,
what time his bow he bent.
To give the struggling spirit a
sweet enfranchisement.
So the death-angel left him,
what time earth's bonds were riven,
The cold, stark, stiffening finger
still pointing up to heaven.

"He had a sore fight of an existence," says Carlyle, "wrestling with Popes and Principalities; in defeat, contention, life-long struggle; rowing as a galley-slave, wandering as an exile. A sore fight: but he won it! 'Have you hope?' they asked him in his last moment, when he could no longer speak. He lifted his finger, pointed upward, and so died! Honour to him! His works have not died. The letter of his work dies, as of all men's; but the spirit of it, never." Did I not say in my opening sentences that John Knox was among the immortal humans? When he entered the world, he came into it for good!

VIII.

"*This* is life eternal, that they might know *Thee!*" "That," says Knox, with his dying breath, "that is where I cast my first anchor!" It is a sure anchorage, O heart of mine! Cast thine anchor there! Cast thine anchor in the oaths and covenants of the Most High! Cast thine anchor in His infallible, immutable, unbreakable Word! Cast thine anchor in the infinite love of God! Cast thine anchor in the redeeming grace of Christ! Cast thine anchor in the everlasting Gospel!

Cast thine anchor in the individual concern of the individual Saviour for the individual soul! Cast thine anchor there; and, come what may, that anchor will always hold!

OLIVER CROMWELL'S TEXT.
(1599-1658)

Oliver Cromwell, a country gentleman and sometimes called the "uncrowned king," was one of England's greatest soldiers and statesmen. He apparently did not become a Christian until he was twenty-four years of age. He adopted the Calvinistic faith and became known in Parliament as a somewhat uncouth Puritan. Early in public life he launched an attack on the bishops. He believed that a Christian could establish direct contact with God through prayer, and that Christian congregations ought to be allowed to choose their own ministers who should serve them by preaching and extemporaneous prayer.

Cromwell became Lord Protector of the republican Commonwealth of England, Scotland, and Ireland from 1653 to 1658. Historians regard him as one who contributed to religious toleration. He strongly opposed severe punishment for minor crimes. Murder, treason, and rebellion alone were subject to capital punishment.

Cromwell was buried in Westminster Abbey, but when Charles II was restored to the throne, his body was hanged and then buried beneath the gallows. A statue of Oliver Cromwell was erected in Westminster in 1899.

His text: "I can do all things through Christ which strengtheneth me" (Philippians 4:13).

I.

OLIVER CROMWELL ranks among the giants. Mr. Frederic Harrison sets his name among the four greatest that our nation has produced. Carlyle's guffaw upon hearing this pretty piece of patronage would have sounded like a thunderclap! Four, indeed! Carlyle would say that the other three would look like a trio of travelling dwarfs grouped about a colossus when they found themselves in the company of Oliver Cromwell. Carlyle can see nothing in our history, nor in any other, more impressive than the spectacle of this young farmer leaving his fields in Huntingdonshire, putting his plough in the shed, and setting out for London to hurl the king from his throne, to dismiss the Parliament, and to reconstitute the country on a new and better basis. He was the one Strong Man; so much stronger than all other men that he bent them to his will and dominated the entire situation. Cromwell made history wholesale. How? That is the question—*How?* And what if, in our search for an answer to that pertinent question, we discover that it was by means of a *text*? Let us go into the matter.

II.

My suspicions in this direction were first aroused by reading a letter that Cromwell wrote to his cousin, Mrs. St. John, before his public career had begun. In this letter he refers to himself as "a poor creature." "I am sure," he says, "that I shall never earn the least mite." Here is strange language for a man who, confident of his resistless strength, will soon be overturning thrones and tossing crowns and kingdoms hither and thither at his pleasure! Is there nothing else in the letter that may help us to elucidate the mystery? There is! He goes on to tell his cousin that, after all, he does not entirely despair of himself. Just one ray of hope has shone upon him, one star has illumined the blackness of his sky. *"One beam in a dark place,"* he says, *"hath much refreshment in it!"* He does not tell his cousin what that ray of hope is; he does not name that solitary star; he does not go into particulars as to that "one beam in a dark place." But we, for our part, must prosecute our investigations until we have discovered it.

III.

It is sometimes best to start at the end of a thing and to work backwards to the beginning. We will adopt that plan in this instance. One who was present at the closing scene has graphically described it for us. "At Hampton Court," he says, "being sick nigh unto death, and in his bed-chamber, Cromwell called for his Bible and desired an honourable and godly person to read unto him that passage in the fourth of Philippians which saith, *'I can do all things through Christ which strengtheneth me.'* Which read, he observed, 'This scripture did once save my life, when my eldest son, poor Robert, died, which went as a dagger to my heart, indeed it did!'"

This does not tell us much; but it sets our feet in the path that may lead to more. And at any rate it makes clear to us what that "one beam" was that so often had much refreshment in it. *"I can do all things through Christ which strengtheneth me."*

IV.

Groping our way back across the years by the aid of the hint given us in those dying words, we come upon that dark and tragic day, nineteen years earlier, when the "son of good promise" died. Unfortunately, the exact circumstances attending the death of the young man have never been recorded. Even the date is shrouded in mystery. Nobody knows in which battle he fell. Perhaps the father was too full of grief and bitterness to write for us that sad and tragic tale. All that we know is what he told us on his deathbed. He says that "it went like a dagger to my heart, indeed it did"; and he says that it brought to his aid the text—the "one beam in a dark place"—that saved his life. It

was not the first time, as we shall
see, that that animating and arousing
word had come, like a relieving
army entering a beleaguered city,
to his deliverance. But the pathos of
that heart-breaking yet heart-healing
experience impressed itself indelibly
upon his memory; the tale was written
in tears; it rushed back upon him as
he lay a-dying; and very often, in the
years that lay between his son's death
and his own, he feelingly referred to
it. In July, 1644, for example, I find
him writing a letter of sympathy to
Colonel Valentine Walton, whose son
has also fallen on the field of battle.
And in this noble yet tender epistle,
Cromwell endeavours to lead the
stricken father to the fountains of
consolation at which he has slaked his
own burning thirst. "Sir," he says,
"God hath taken away your eldest son
by a cannon-shot. You know my own
trials this way, but the Lord supported
me. I remembered that my boy had

entered into the happiness we all pant for and live for. There, too, is your precious child, full of glory, never to know sin or sorrow any more. He was a gallant young man, exceedingly gracious. God give you His comfort! *You may do all things through Christ which strengtheneth us.* Seek that, and you shall easily bear your trial. The Lord be your strength!"

"*I can do all things through Christ which strengtheneth me!*"

"*This scripture,*" he says, as he lies upon his deathbed, "*did once save my life!*"

"*Seek that!*" he says to Colonel Walton, "*seek that! seek that!*"

V.

But we must go back further yet. We are tracing the stream, but we have not reached the fountainhead. That deathbed testimony at Hampton Court was delivered in 1658. It was in

1639, or thereabouts, that Robert, his eldest son, was lying dead. On each of these occasions the text wonderfully supported him. But, in each case, it came to him as an old friend and not as a new acquaintance. For it was in 1638—the year before Robert's death and twenty years before the father's—that Cromwell wrote to his cousin, Mrs. St. John, about the "one beam in a dark place that hath such exceedingly great refreshment in it." When, then, did that beam break upon his darksome path for the first time?

Carlyle thinks that it was in 1623. Cromwell was then in his twenty-fourth year, with all his life before him. But we may as well let Carlyle speak for himself. "At about this time took place," he says, "what Cromwell, with unspeakable joy, would name his conversion. Certainly a grand epoch for a man; properly the one epoch; the turning-point which guides upwards, or guides downwards, him and his activities for evermore! Wilt thou join with the Dragons; wilt thou join with the Gods? Oliver was henceforth a Christian man; believed in God, not on Sundays only, but on all days, in all places, and in all cases."

In 1623 it was, then: but how? Piecing the scraps together, a mere hint here and a vague suggestion there, I gather that it was somewhat in this way. In 1623 all things were rushing pellmell towards turgid crisis, wild tumult and red revolution. At home and abroad the outlook was as black as black could be. The world wanted a man, a good man, a great man, a strong man, to save it. Everybody saw the need; but nobody could see the man. Down in Huntingdonshire a young farmer leans on the handles of his plough.

"The world needs a man, a good man, a great man, a strong man!" says his Reason. And then he hears another voice.

"Thou art the man!" cries his Conscience, with terrifying suddenness; and his hands tremble as they grasp the plough.

That evening, as he sits beside the fire, his young wife opposite him, and little Robert in the cot by his side, he takes down his Bible and reads. He turns to the epistle to the Philippians, at the closing chapter. He is amazed at the things that, by the grace divine, Paul claims to have learned and achieved.

"It's true, Paul," he exclaims, "that *you* have learned this and attained to this measure of grace; but what shall *I* do? Ah, poor creature, it is a hard, hard lesson for me to take out! I find it so!"

Poring over the sacred volume, however, he makes the discovery of his lifetime. "I came," he says, "to the thirteenth verse, where Paul saith, *'I can do all things through Christ which strengtheneth me.'* Then faith began to work, and my heart to find comfort and support; and I said to myself, 'He that was *Paul's* Christ is *my* Christ too!' And so I drew water out of the Wells of Salvation!"

And now we have reached the fountain-head at last!

VI.

And so the clodhopper became the king! It was *the text* that did it! Considered apart from the text, the life of Cromwell is an insoluble mystery, a baffling enigma. But take one good look at the text: observe the place that it occupied in Cromwell's heart and thought: and everything becomes plain. "That such a man, with the eye to see and with the heart to dare, should advance, from post to post, from victory to victory, till the Huntingdon Farmer became, by whatever name you call him, the acknowledged Strongest Man in England, virtually the King of

England, requires," says Carlyle, "no magic to explain it." Of course not! The text explains it. For see!

What is a king? In his *French Revolution*, Carlyle says that the very word "king" comes from Kon-ning Can-ning, the Man Who Can, the Man Who is Able! And that is precisely the burden of the text.

"I can do all things through Christ which strengtheneth me"; so the Authorised Version has it.

"In Him who strengthens me I am able for anything"; so Dr. Moffatt translates the words.

"For all things I am strong in Him who makes me able"; thus Bishop Moule renders it.

A King, says Carlyle, is an Able Man, a Strong Man, a Man who Can. Here is a ploughman who sees that the world is perishing for want of just such a King. How can he, weak as he is, become the world's Strong Man, the world's Able Man, the world's King? The text tells him.

"I can do all things," he cries, *"through Him that strengtheneth me!"*

The Strong Man was made and the world was saved.

VII.

A man—at any rate such a man as Cromwell—can never be content to enjoy such an experience as this alone. No man can read the Life or Letters of the Protector without being touched by his solicitude for others. He is for ever anxious that his kindred and friends should drink of those wondrous waters that have so abundantly refreshed and invigorated him. After quoting his text to Colonel Walton, he urges him to seek that same strengthening grace which he himself has received.

"Seek that!" he says; *"seek that!"*

It is the keynote of all his correspondence. "I hope," he writes to the Mayor of Hursley in 1650, "I hope you give my son good counsel;

I believe he needs it. He is in the dangerous time of his age, and it is a very vain world. O how good it is to close with Christ betimes! There is nothing else worth looking after!"

"Seek that strength!" he says to Colonel Walton.

"Seek that Saviour!" he says to his wayward son.

"Seek that which will really satisfy!" he says to his daughter.

It always seems to me that the old Puritan's lovely letter to that daughter of his, the letter from which I have just quoted, is the gem of Carlyle's great volume. Bridget was twenty-two at the time. "Your sister," her father tells her, "is exercised with some perplexed thoughts. She sees her own vanity and carnal mind, and bewailing it, she seeks after what will satisfy. And thus to be a seeker is to be of the best sect next to a finder, and such an one shall every faithful humble seeker be at the end. Happy seeker; happy finder!

Dear heart, press on! Let not husband, let not anything cool thy affections after Christ!"

With which strong, tender, fatherly words from the old soldier to his young daughter we may very well take our leave of him.

BLAISE PASCAL'S TEXT.
(1623-1662)

Blaise Pascal was a French religious philosopher, a mathematician, physicist, and mystic. An accident in 1654, in which he almost lost his life, brought him to a genuine conversion experience. His doctrine centered on the person of Christ and that one can experience God only through the heart rather than reason.

Pascal's work Pensées, *a treatise on spirituality, has been translated into many languages. In English, it is simply known as* Thoughts. *He also wrote a series of nineteen letters published under the title* Provincial Letters of Pascal, *in which he comes out as a champion of freedom of conscience, of truth, and of justice against the powerful Jesuits of his day.*

His text: "For my people have committed two evils: they have forsaken Me, the fountain of living waters, and hewed them out cisterns, broken cisterns, that can hold no water" (Jeremiah 2:13).

I.

THE conversion of Blaise Pascal is one of the shining events in the stately history of the Christian Church. Seldom has so mighty an intellect submitted with such perfect grace to the authority of the Saviour. Pascal is not only one of the world's epoch-makers; he is one of the architects of civilization. Every day of our lives we all of us do things that, but for Pascal, we could never have done. Every day of our lives we enjoy comforts and privileges that, but for him, could never have been ours. His commanding personality and triumphant reason dominate human life at every turn. He is one of history's quiet conquerors; he does not advertise himself; his work does not lend itself to parade or display; yet, put him among the giants of the past, and most of them are instantly dwarfed by his presence. Few names, as Principal Tulloch says, are more classical than his. "Though cut off at the early age of thirty-nine, there is hardly any name more famous at once in literature, science and religion." For three centuries every thinker of note has been profoundly influenced by him. The annals of France glitter with a multitude of brilliant personalities; but none of them shine with a lustre that is comparable to that of Pascal.

II.

He was only a youth when he shook the dust of the world from his feet and entered upon the life of a lay solitary at Port Royal; yet the amazing thing is that, by that time, he had established a reputation for mathematical audacity, philosophical originality, and scientific ingenuity which no record in the world's long history can rival. He was,

Bossuet says, endowed by God with all the gifts of understanding; a geometer of the first rank; a profound logician, a lofty and eloquent writer. If, Bossuet maintains, we scan a list of his inventions and discoveries, and then reflect that, in addition, he wrote one of the most perfect works that has ever appeared in the French language, and that in all his books there are passages of unrivalled eloquence and depth of reflection, we shall come to the conclusion that a greater genius never existed in any country or in any age. Again and again, whilst Pascal was a mere boy, Paris was electrified by his dazzling discoveries. As one reads the romantic and almost incredible story of those early years, it is impossible to repress a conjecture as to the part that he would have played in the history of the world, and the sensational changes that he would have effected, *if* he had persisted in the career to which he devoted his earlier years, and *if* he had been spared to old age in the pursuit of those researches.

The bent of his mind betrayed itself as soon as he was out of his cradle. Like John Stuart Mill, he was educated by his father. Like the elder Mill, the elder Pascal had ideas of his own concerning the intellectual development and ultimate career of his boy. But there is an essential difference between the two cases. John Stuart Mill loyally adopted his father's ideas and dutifully followed the path that had been prepared for his feet. Blaise Pascal, on the contrary, rebelled against the programme mapped out for him, and eventually brought his father to his own way of thinking.

The elder Pascal was obsessed by one all-mastering prejudice. He was determined, come what might, that his boy should have nothing to do with mathematics. He was himself a mathematician, and experience had taught him that the study of mathematics captivates and monopolises the mind to the exclusion of all other themes. He therefore set himself to guard his son's mind from all contact with mathematical lore. Every book that touched on mathematical problems was carefully concealed in the presence of the boy; the father abstained from discussing mathematical topics with his friends; and, to make matters absolutely secure, the father set his son such difficult lessons in Latin and other languages as would leave him neither time nor energy nor inclination for the speculations that he so ardently desired him to eschew. But, in all this, the elder Pascal resembles nothing so much as an anxious hen frantically endeavouring to teach her brood of ducklings to avoid the water towards which all the instincts of their nature are impelling them.

III.

As a child Pascal was characterized by an extraordinary and insatiable curiosity. It was not merely the passive curiosity that smiles, wonders, and passes on: it was the active curiosity that insists on investigating the why and the wherefore of each arresting circumstance and phenomenon. He was little more than an infant when he noticed that a plate, struck with a knife, emits a loud and lingering sound; but that, as soon as a hand is laid upon it, the sound instantly ceases. Every child has noticed this, and has been interested and amused by it: but the matter has ended there. Pascal, however, immediately initiated a series of experiments based upon this curious happening. *Why* did the knife awaken the sound? *Why* did the fingers silence it? The boy was soon working out a philosophy of sounds. His father had forbidden his meddling with geometry in any form; but the temptation was too great. In the secrecy of his own room he kept a supply of charcoal and a few boards. On these he practised making circles that should be perfectly round, triangles whose angles should be exactly equal, and other figures of the kind. Working away by himself, he came, quite independently, to many of the conclusions elaborated by Euclid. On one such occasion, the father crept into the room on tiptoe. The boy was so engrossed in his demonstrations that for some time he was unaware of his father's presence. The father stood for a while dumbfounded. He felt as the hen may be supposed to feel when she sees the ducklings well out on the pond. He recognised that the boy was in his element. Startled by the brilliance of his son's genius, he left the room without saying a word. And, with a wisdom that does him credit, he strode off to the city to secure for the youth teachers who would be able to assist him along the line for which he had so obvious a bent.

At the age of sixteen, Pascal wrote his famous treatise on Conic Sections. The most brilliant Frenchmen of the time were staggered. With one accord they declared that it was the most powerful and valuable contribution that had been made to mathematical science since the days of Archimedes. Whilst still in his 'teens, Pascal made up his mind that science, to fulfil its destiny, must relate itself to the industry and commerce of the workaday world. Acting on this principle, he began by inventing a calculating machine and finished by inventing, on his deathbed, the commonplace but useful vehicle that we now call an omnibus. The difficulties involved in the construction of the calculating machine prevented its being of much use to his own generation; but, later on, those obstacles were overcome, and the contrivance of Pascal paved the way for all the cash registers and adding-machines of our modern shops and offices. But perhaps the greatest triumph of Pascal's genius was his discovery that atmosphere has definite weight, and that the level of the mercury varies in different altitudes and different weather. Sir David Brewster has given us a vivid and amusing description of the experiments made by Pascal first at the base, and then at the summit, of the Puy-de-Dome on the memorable day on which he established his historic conclusions. On that day— Saturday, September 19, 1648—Pascal virtually gave us the barometer, and thus made a contribution to the science of meteorology which it is impossible now to overvalue. This triumph led him to his prolonged series of researches concerning the equilibrium of fluids; and there are those who regard his treatise on this subject as his crowning achievement. But, however that may be, there he stands! He is still in the twenties; yet all the world knows him as a thinker of unsurpassed brilliance and audacity; as a scientist who knows how to harness the most profound erudition to the most practical ends; and as a writer who can express the most abstruse ideas in language that a little child can understand.

IV.

The greatest day in Pascal's life was the day of his conversion. Except in the light of that momentous happening, his biography is unintelligible. As Dean Church puts it, the religion of Pascal is essentially the religion of a converted man. He was thirty-one at the time; and so overwhelming was the flood-tide of divine grace that came surging into his heart that, to the day of his death, he wore stitched into his doublet, a piece of parchment on which he had recorded the exact hour of that unforgettable experience. It was *in the year of grace 1654, on Monday the twenty-third of November, from half-past ten in the evening until half an hour after midnight.*

Yet whilst in one sense, that conversion of his was so sudden and cataclysmic that he can chronicle with the utmost definiteness the precise moment at which it took place, there is *another* sense in which it was very gradual. I can trace its slow development. Eight years earlier, in 1646, a number of excellent books had fallen into his hands. This course of reading so affected him, his sister tells us, that he came to the conclusion that, to be a Christian, man ought to live only for God and to seek no object but His pleasure. "This became so evident to my brother, and so imperative, that he relinquished for a time all his scientific researches and set himself to seek that *one thing needful* of which our Lord has spoken."

Having once applied himself to this sublime quest, he kept his eyes wide open. The most arresting object on his horizon was the exquisite beauty of his sister's life. In earlier days, *his* studious ways had rebuked her frivolity and led her to seriousness: now *her* devotion shames his worldliness. She led a life of such sweetness, unselfishness, and charm that her very presence was a perpetual benediction on everybody in the house. It was a poignant grief to her to see her brother, to whom she felt that she owed the grace that she herself enjoyed, bemoaning the destitution of his own soul. She saw him frequently, pitied him increasingly, and pleaded with him to abandon everything that clogged his spirit and to yield himself without reserve to the Saviour.

The momentous crisis was precipitated at length by accident. "One day," says Bossuet, "when he went to take his daily drive to the bridge of Neuilly in a carriage and four, the two leading horses became restive at a point at which the road was bounded by a parapet over the river. They reared and plunged and eventually, to the horror of the onlookers, flung themselves over the stonework into the Seine. Fortunately, the first strokes of their feet broke the traces which bound them to the pole, and the carriage hung suspended on the brink of the parapet. The effect of such a shock to a man of Pascal's feeble health may be imagined. He swooned away and was restored only with difficulty. His nerves were so shattered that, long afterwards, during sleepless nights and moments of weakness, he seemed to see a precipice at his bedside over which he was on the point of falling." This happened in October, 1654; a month later he found joy and peace in believing. "On the night of the twenty-third of November," says Madame Duclaux, "he found himself unable to sleep, and lay in bed reading the Scriptures. Suddenly his eyes dazzled; a flame of fire seemed to envelop him. Such a moment of marvellous euphoria could never be forgotten, and, in mortal words, could never be expressed. It found natural utterance in floods of tears and in that fragmentary speech which, like so many sobs, Pascal employs in that mystic Memorial which thenceforth he ever wore in secret, sewn into his clothes like a talisman. Here it is:

FIRE!
Certainty! Joy! Peace!
I forget the world and everything but God!
Righteous Father, the world hath
not known Thee, but I have known Thee!
Joy, Joy, Joy! Tears of Joy!
Jesus! Jesus!
I separated myself from Him;
renounced and crucified Him!
They have forsaken ME,
the fountain of living waters!
I separated myself from HIM!

May I not be separated from Him eternally!
I submit myself absolutely to
JESUS CHRIST MY REDEEMER.

In that hour, Blaise Pascal, the mightiest thinker of his time, was converted! "All in a moment," as Viscount St. Cyres puts it, "he was touched by God. He was caught in the grip of a mysterious Power. Some strange spiritual chemistry blotted out his former tastes and inclinations and left him a new being." He himself called it his conversion; and, in order that others might share with him the rapture of so radiant an experience, he sat down almost at once and wrote his treatise *On the Conversion of the Sinner.* And, if ever we are tempted to suppose that his fire-baptism was simply one moment of frenzy punctuating a life of scholarly frigidity, we are confronted by the significant circumstance that, to his dying day, he wore the Memorial next to his heart.

He was loyal to his vision to the end. "And so," he wrote, when nearing his goal, "and so I stretch forth my hands to my Redeemer, who came to earth to suffer and to die for me." In that faith so simple yet so sublime—so personal yet so profound—Pascal rested serenely to the last.

My people have committed two evils: they have forsaken Me, the fountain of living waters, and hewed out to themselves cisterns, broken cisterns, that can hold no water. This is the passage that was running in Pascal's mind that November midnight; and he inscribed it across the very centre of his historic Memorial.

"His eyes had been opened," says Dean Church. "He felt himself touched and overcome by the greatness and the reasonableness of things unseen. He consciously turned to God, not from vice, but from the bondage of the interests of time, from the fascination of a merely intellectual life and from the frivolity which forgets the other world in this."

Here then are *the cisterns, the broken cisterns that can hold no water*—"the bondage of the interests of time; from the fascination of a merely intellectual life; the frivolity which forgets the other world in this!"

And here is *the fountain of living waters* that he for so long forsook! Jesus! Jesus! Jesus! Jesus Christ my Redeemer! From that November midnight, Jesus was everything to Pascal—*everything!* "His whole argument," says Viscount St. Cyres, "centres in the person of the Redeemer." "To him," says Principal Tulloch, "Christ was the only solution of all human perplexities." From the age of thirty-one to the day of his death, at the age of thirty-nine, he had but one desire: he lived that he might turn the thoughts of his fellow men to his Saviour.

It may be that, during those last

years of his brief life, he devoted less time to science, although, as his biographers are careful to show, he by no means relinquished it. But, as against this, we must remember that, during those closing years, he wrote a book that will be treasured as long as the world stands. Lord Avebury included it in his list of the best books ever written. And nobody has read Pascal's *Thoughts* without being lifted by it into a clearer atmosphere and helped to a loftier plane.

Blaise Pascal was endowed with a soul of singularly delicate texture. He had a mind that was amazingly sensitive to all those vibrations by which truth reveals itself to men; he had an eye that was quick to see beauty in whatever form it presented itself; he had a heart that insistently hungered for the sublime. In his early days he saw the *High* and it entranced him; but on that never-to-be-forgotten November night, he saw the *Highest*.

Without reserve and without delay he laid all his marvellous faculties of heart and brain at the feet of the Saviour who, that night, had revealed Himself in such a bewildering wealth of power and grace.

The End.

BOOKS BY A.L.O.E.

THE BATTLE (Sequel to *The Giant Killer*)

DASHED TO PIECES

ESCAPE FROM THE EAGLE'S NEST

EXILES IN BABYLON *(Heroes of Faith Series)*

THE GIANT KILLER

THE GOLDEN FLEECE

THE HAUNTED ROOM

HEBREW HEROES

THE JEWEL

NED FRANKS: THE ONE-ARMED SAILOR

THE PASSAGE

THE PILGRIM'S CALL

PRIDE AND HIS PRISONERS

RESCUED FROM EGYPT *(Heroes of Faith Series)*

THE ROBBERS' CAVE

THE SHEPHERD OF BETHLEHEM *(Heroes of Faith Series)*

TRIUMPH OVER MIDIAN *(Heroes of Faith Series)*

THE WANDERER IN AFRICA

A.L.O.E. (1821-1893) was born Charlotte Maria Tucker near Barnet, Middlesex, England. She was the sixth child of her parents and was educated at home. Under the pseudonym A.L.O.E. (A Lady of England), she wrote over 140 books for children, most with an obvious moral, and devoted the proceeds to charity. In 1875, she left England for India and spent the rest of her life there, engaged in missionary work.

1-888-A-GOSPEL • 1-888-246-7735

BOOKS BY
MRS. O.F. WALTON

CHRISTIE, THE KING'S SERVANT
CHRISTIE'S OLD ORGAN
LITTLE FAITH
THE LOST CLUE
MY MATES AND I
A PEEP BEHIND THE SCENES
SAVED AT SEA
THROW ME OVERBOARD
WHEN YOU LEAST EXPECT IT
WINTER'S FOLLY

MRS. O.F. WALTON (1849-1939) was born Amy Catherine Deck in Kent, England. Shortly after her marriage to Octavius Frank Walton, the couple moved to Jerusalem, where Octavius ministered in a church on Mount Zion and Amy wrote *A Peep Behind the Scenes*. Her book *Christie's Old Organ* was one of the earliest books in history of both Christian and children's literature to be translated and published in Japan.

WWW.LAMPLIGHTER.NET

Books by
Christoph von Schmid

The Basket of Flowers
The Bird's Nest
The Captive
Fire in the Sky
The Inheritance
The Little Lamb
The Lost Ruby
The Painted Fly and Other Stories
Rosa of Linden Castle
Schmid's Tales
The White Dove
Worth More Than Gold

Christoph von Schmid (1768-1854) was born in Bavaria, studied theology, and became an ordained priest in 1791. In 1796 he was placed at the head of a large school, where he began writing stories for children, reading them after school hours as a reward, on condition that the children would write the stories down at home. In 1841, he published a complete edition of his scattered writings in 24 volumes. He is considered the pioneer writer of books for children, and his stories have been translated into at least 24 languages.

1-888-A-GOSPEL • 1-888-246-7735

Books by Amy Le Feuvre

Amy Le Feuvre (1861-1929) was born in London, England, and grew up in a large family. She was a prolific author of children's books with a strong Christian message. Her book *Teddy's Button* was one of the most popular of all late Victorian children's stories.

BOOKS OF THE YEAR

Books of the Year are determined by biblical insights, captivating plots, and life-changing character lessons.

1-888-A-GOSPEL • 1-888-246-7735

ILLUSTRATED BOOKS

We are delighted to present to you this creative collection with beautiful illustrations for young visual learners. Reinforce character building and stimulate imagination with our Illustrated Collection. To view the complete collection, visit *www.lamplighter.net*.

TRUSTY: TRIED AND TRUE
Written by Mark Hamby, *Really* written by Debbie Hamby
Illustrated by Jennifer Brandon

THIS adorable adventure is bursting with colorful imagery to heighten a child's imagination and stir creativity. Learn about selfishness, pride, and vanity through the characters of Brawny, Smarty, and Beauty, and be inspired by our hero Trusty, who courageously tries to help. This will surely become a family favorite to be read over and over again!

THE THREE WEAVERS, ILLUSTRATED
Rewritten by Mark Hamby
Illustrated by Jennifer Brandon

A DELIGHTFUL allegory for fathers to read with their daughters—not just once, but over and over again. This illustrated rendition reveals how each weaver prepares his daughter to weave a mantle perfectly suited for the prince. But each father uses a different approach, and the consequences are very revealing! Enjoy many thought-provoking conversations, creating memories for years to come.

LAMPLIGHTER THEATRE

Lamplighter Theatre helps to fulfill the mission of Lamplighter by bringing redemptive hope to the world through dramatic audio. Forged through the commitment and sacrifice of a dedicated team, Lamplighter Theatre now airs on 1800 radio stations in 29 countries.

SIR MALCOLM AND THE MISSING PRINCE
2-DISC AUDIO DRAMA

Inside the castle walls a battle rages in the heart of a widowed king. His son, the young Prince Hubert, has proven himself to be an unworthy heir to the throne. But a bold intervention by the king's most trusted knight could prove to be the cure. In the remote lands of this vast kingdom, far from the walls of the palace, Hugh will learn that the requirement of kingship is servanthood. *Best for ages 6-11.*

Approximate Time: 2 hrs.

FROZEN FIRE
2-DISC AUDIO DRAMA

The events that lead up to Betty's pivotal decision demonstrate the true meaning of humility, servanthood, and love. Inspired by a true story, Betty must come face to face with a dreaded foe. Facing myriad trials, including

abandonment and the death-grip of a terrifying blizzard, her love for her devoted servant trumps all. You will fall in love with Betty, whose loyalty is demonstrated through tremendous courage and sacrifice. *Frozen Fire* will keep you on the edge of your seat! Great for the entire family.

Approximate Time: 2 hrs.

Learn more, listen to samples, and view entire drama collection at

WWW.LAMPLIGHTER.NET

Best For...

The 'Best For' Collections are designed for those individuals who have seen this engaging collection of books and wondered which would be best for their children. We have selected an array of stories for each age group to give you just a taste of what Lamplighter books are all about.

Best For Ages 6-11

Basil; or, Honesty and Industry

Christie's Old Organ

The Giant Killer

Helen's Temper

Jack the Conqueror

Jessica's First Prayer

Jill's Red Bag

Joseph's Shield

Little Sir Galahad

Little Threads

Probable Sons

Teddy's Button

The White Dove

Best For Ages 9-14

The Basket of Flowers

The Captive

The Golden Thread

The Hedge of Thorns

The Little Lamb

My Golden Ship

Hand on the Bridle

A Peep Behind the Scenes

Rising to the Top

The Robbers' Cave

Rosa of Linden Castle

Shipwrecked, But Not Lost

Trapped Beneath the Surface

The White Knights

Best For Ages 12-99

The Alabaster Box

Escape from the Eagle's Nest

The Haunted Room

The Hidden Hand

Ishmael

The Lamplighter

The Lost Clue

Sir Knight of the
    Splendid Way

The White Gypsy

WWW.LAMPLIGHTER.NET

my LAMPLIGHTER
BOOK & AUDIO CLUB

The *myLamplighter Book Club* allows you to follow your own personalized strategic plan as you make a wise investment for your family. We are offering you the opportunity to own the entire Lamplighter collection at your own pace, so that you are in control of your investment.

- SIMPLICITY – YOU choose which titles you would like to receive each month.
- SAVINGS – YOU decide how much money you'd like to save each month!
- CONVENIENCE – YOU maintain and update your account anytime, anywhere.

You can switch plans or temporarily put your club on hold.
You can remove titles from your queue.
You can update and maintain your account online.
Shipping is FREE! *Book Club is not offered outside the US.*
Membership is FREE!
Character Comprehension Quizzes are FREE - $199 value!

PLAN 1	**1 Book per month**
PLAN 2	**2 Books per month**
PLAN 3	**3 Books per month**
PLAN 4	**4 Books per month**

TO SIGN UP...
Log in at *www.lamplighter.net/book-audio-club.*

1-888-A-GOSPEL • 1-888-246-7735

THE
LAMPLIGHTER MISSION

Printing books of high quality with an emphasis on character development, biblical insights, artistic design, excellence, and skilled craftsmanship is an integral part of the Lamplighter Mission. Guided by our mission "to make ready a people prepared for the Lord" (Luke 1:17), Lamplighter Publishing and Bindery is strategically engaged by building Christlike character one story at a time. Through the mystery and adventure of Lamplighter stories, the framework of character development is formed and the pursuit of excellence is cultivated. The dominant theme of hope is developed by characters who persevere in adversity, being fully convinced that nothing is impossible with God.

It is the Lamplighter commitment that each book instills moral values through role models that either demonstrate exemplary behavior or suffer the consequences of making wrong choices. A riveting plot, a worthy theme, and endearing characters will motivate readers, both young and old, to adopt a similar moral code by emulating the characters that have now been etched into their awakened conscience.

The goal of Lamplighter Ministries is to cultivate a renaissance of creative excellence that inspires one to know God intimately and proclaim Him passionately. At the Lamplighter Guild, students have the opportunity to work alongside world-class actors, scriptwriters, sound designers, music composers, oil painters, theologians, culinary artists, and other master teachers.

Through these masters, Lamplighter Theatre was established, providing a platform from which Lamplighter books are adapted into classic audio dramas now aired in 29 countries. Lamplighter Ministries stands on the shoulders of those who have built a good foundation. It is our commitment to remain faithful to these high standards and inspire others to do the same and more. In the words of Solomon, "Do you see a man skillful in his work? He will stand before kings; he will not stand before obscure men" (Proverbs 22:29).

*For more information about
Lamplighter Ministries,
visit www.lamplighter.net
or www.lamplighterguild.com.
To order a free catalog go to
www.lamplighter.net or call toll free
1-888-A-GOSPEL (1-888-246-7735).*

LAMPLIGHTER Publishing

BUILDING CHRISTLIKE CHARACTER ... ONE STORY AT A TIME

FASTENED LIKE NAILS, VOLUME 1.

FLESCH-KINKAID GRADE LEVEL: 6.3

BIBLICAL INSIGHTS: PP. 9, 12, 25, 34, 43, 51, 61, 66, 80, 83, 95, 111.

CHARACTER TRAITS: love for God's Word, faith, perseverance

To request a catalog, please contact us:
Phone: 1-888-A-GOSPEL (1-888-246-7735)
or 1-570-585-1314
Email: *mail@lamplighter.net*
or visit our website at *www.lamplighter.net*.

ISBN 978-1-58474-247-0

9 781584 742470 >